*The Lay of the Love and Death
of Cornet Christopher Rilke*

RILKE was born in Prague in 1875, the son of a conventional army-officer father and a religious-fanatical mother, who first sent him, most unsuitably, to military school. After that, largely autodidact, he studied philosophy, history, literature, art, in Prague, Munich, Berlin. From his earliest years he wrote verse. In the '90s both *Erste* and *Frühe Gedichte* appeared, short stories, plays. Much of his early work he declined to include in his collected works. In 1899 (which saw the *Cornet*, first version) came the first of two trips to Russia with Lou Andreas-Salomé (*Vom lieben Gott und Anderes*, later to be called *Geschichten vom Lieben Gott*, appeared in December 1900). He married Clara Westhoff in 1901, lived in Worpswede till the birth of their only child, Ruth, moving to Paris in 1902, Clara to work with Rodin, Rilke to write his monograph on him. Between travels in Germany, France, Italy, Spain, Egypt, Scandinavia, and his prodigious letter-writing, the twelve years with Paris as base were productive: *Stundenbuch, Buch der Bilder, Neue Gedichte, Notebooks of M. L. Brigge*, translations of E. B. Browning, Gide, de Guérin. After the outbreak of World War I he lived mostly in Munich, served briefly in army office work in Vienna, and in 1919 went to Switzerland. Here, in the small stone tower of Muzot, he achieved in 1922 the *Duineser Elegien* and the *Sonette an Orpheus*, followed by poems in French and translations of Valéry and others. He died at Valmont near Glion on December 29, 1926, and is buried beside the little church of Raron overlooking the Rhone Valley.

RAINER MARIA RILKE

In Translations by M. D. HERTER NORTON
Letters to a Young Poet
Sonnets to Orpheus
Wartime Letters of Rainer Maria Rilke
Translations from the Poetry of Rainer Maria Rilke
The Lay of the Love and Death of Cornet Christopher Rilke
The Notebooks of Malte Laurids Brigge
Stories of God

Translated by STEPHEN SPENDER and J. B. LEISHMAN
Duino Elegies

Translated by JANE BANNARD GREENE and M. D. HERTER NORTON
Letters of Rainer Maria Rilke
Volume One, 1892–1910   Volume Two, 1910–1926

THE LAY OF THE LOVE AND DEATH OF CORNET CHRISTOPHER RILKE

RAINER MARIA RILKE

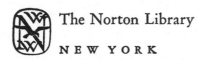

The Norton Library

NEW YORK

W·W·NORTON & COMPANY·INC·

FIRST PUBLISHED IN THE NORTON LIBRARY 1963

ISBN 0 393 00159 8

W. W. Norton & Company, Inc. also publishes *The Norton Anthology of English Literature*, edited by M. H. Abrams et al; *The Norton Anthology of Poetry*, edited by Arthur M. Eastman et al; *World Masterpieces*, edited by Maynard Mack et al; *The Norton Reader*, edited by Arthur M. Eastman et al; *The Norton Facsimile of the First Folio of Shakespeare*, prepared by Charlton Hinman; *The Norton Anthology of Modern Poetry*, edited by Richard Ellmann and Robert O'Clair; and the *Norton Critical Editions*.

PRINTED IN THE UNITED STATES OF AMERICA

67890

Translation by
M. D. HERTER NORTON

A few revisions have been made in the present translation, first published in 1932. The German text is taken from Volume I (1955) of the definitive edition by Dr. Ernst Zinn of *Rainer Maria Rilke, Sämtliche Werke*, Insel-Verlag (Zweigstelle Wiesbaden).

Foreword   The *Cornet* is an early work, written in Schmargendorf (Berlin) in 1899. According to Rilke's own account, it was set down "all in one night"—an autumn night of moon and cloud, by the light of a couple of windblown candles. In the back of his mind was a document, a copy of which had recently come to his attention among some family papers, concerning a young Rilke fallen in Hungary in 1663 in a campaign against the Turks. Only this was history, the rest his own romantic invention.

The little work was not published until 1904, in the October issue of the Prag periodical *Deutsche Arbeit*, after Rilke had revised it somewhat during his stay that summer at Borgeby Gård in Sweden. Once again, in 1906, this time for book publication, he carefully "recast and tested" the text, and this final version appeared toward the end of that year. Addressing himself to this task not long after he had left Rodin—in other words, in the first freedom of his artistic maturity—he expressed his feeling that it was a very youthful work "calling for much forgiveness" (To Clara Rilke, May 25, 1906).

He had little inkling of the popularity in store for it. In 1912 Insel-Verlag, who had taken it over from the original publisher, brought it out as the first in a new series of *Fünfzig-Pfennig-Bücher* (*Fifty-Cent Books*), as they were then called, soon to grow into the famous *Inselbücherei*. By August there was need for further printings; *The Cornet* had sold 8,000 copies in three weeks. "My dear friend", Rilke wrote Anton Kippenberg on the 3rd of that month, "How well you have mounted this good

Christopher Rilke. Who would have thought it?"

Five years later, when a first edition of *New Poems* not yet out of print had brought 370 marks at an auction, the "old Cornet", then in its 140th thousand and steadily continuing, brought three times that amount: "people are simply crazy in this respect too", Rilke wrote his wife (To Clara Rilke, November 4th, 1917). In 1956 the printings had run to some 950,000.

In the 1920's translations began to appear, in Italy, France, England, America, South America. Some editions have, of course, been illustrated. And it has more than once been set to music, a combination of arts for which the author himself had little sympathy.

In November of 1914 Rilke heard "a singularly moving story [which, however, he does not tell] from an officer of Hussars, who was among the first to be wounded before Longwy . . . and the Cornet is touchingly interwoven with it all . . . " (To Clara Rilke, November 18, 1914). And again in 1915: "I quite unexpectedly find myself among the authors of this exceptional year, my voice of fifteen years ago speaks into the attentive ear of the people who for months have been frightened—my voice? The voice of that one distant night of my youth in which I wrote the Cornet, incited to it by clouds passing in strange flight across the moon . . . " (To Thankmar von Münchhausen, March 6th, 1915). Even in the Second World War *The Cornet* went to the front in various pockets of the new soldiery. A French officer tells of finding a copy in a German dugout in the Sarre in 1939, lying on a rough deal stand together with a revolver, a telephone and a table of logarithms . . . .

Rilke's writing lays an obligation upon its translator to work, as far as possible, as he himself worked: with simple words, for a finely-sentient clarity, and furthermore with rhythmic pulse alert and an always listening ear, testing the sound of the language—word, verse, line —even to its last vanishing ring. This is not an easy task; It needs time, and an aura of silence. But it would seem that a simple, very close adherence to the original most justly conveys the quality of Rilke's style, and that his German and our English language are not so unrelated as to make this altogether impossible.

One deliberate exception concerns the matter of rhyme, conspicuously in the 11th and 24th vignettes, and also in certain others. Here the rhymes which run naturally in German become sought-for in English and have no implicit spontaneity. Generally, in achieving rhyme, the new language inserts words not in the original, diluting the expression and changing the rhythmic emphasis, both of which results are detrimental to the style and spirit. Rilke's rhymed metre is subtle, he slips into it without apparent effort; and its effect is better paralleled by an unrhymed literal translation cast in the necessary swing than by lines strained and altered for the sake of rhyme.

The translator must do his very best, and then apologize for doing it at all. Even his intent is presumptuous. But this little prose-poem, beloved of so many thousands not only in Germany, has proved to have a universal appeal that transcends language.

M.D.H.N.

Die Weise von Liebe und Tod
des Cornets Christoph Rilke

*The Lay of the Love and Death
of Cornet Christopher Rilke*

"*...den 24. November 1663 wurde Otto von Rilke / auf Langenau / Gränitz und Ziegra / zu Linda mit seines in Ungarn gefallenen Bruders Christoph hinterlassenem Antheile am Gute Linda beliehen; doch musste er einen Revers ausstellen / nach welchem die Lehensreichung null und nichtig sein sollte / im Falle sein Bruder Christoph (der nach beigebrachtem Totenschein als Cornet in der Compagnie des Freiherrn von Pirovano des kaiserl.oesterr. Heysterschen Regiments zu Ross . . . verstorben war) zurückkehrt . . .*"

"... the 24th of November 1663 Otto von Rilke / of Langenau /
Gränitz and Ziegra / at Linda was enfeoffed with the share of
the Linda estate left by his brother Christopher, fallen in
Hungary: but he had to make out a reversion / by which the
feudal tenure would become null and void / in case his brother
Christopher (who according to the death certificate presented had
died as Cornet in the Baron of Pirovano's Company of the
Imperial Austrian Heyster Regiment of Horse ...)
should return ...."

*R*eiten, *reiten*, reiten, durch den Tag, durch die Nacht, durch den Tag.

Reiten, reiten, reiten.

Und der Mut ist so müde geworden und die Sehnsucht so gross. Es gibt keine Berge mehr, kaum einen Baum. Nichts wagt aufzustehen. Fremde Hütten hocken durstig an versumpften Brunnen. Nirgends ein Turm. Und immer das gleiche Bild. Man hat zwei Augen zuviel. Nur in der Nacht manchmal glaubt man den Weg zu kennen. Vielleicht kehren wir nächtens immer wieder das Stück zurück, das wir in der fremden Sonne mühsam gewonnen haben? Es kann sein. Die Sonne ist schwer, wie bei uns tief im Sommer. Aber wir haben im Sommer Abschied genommen. Die Kleider der Frauen leuchteten lang aus dem Grün. Und nun reiten wir lang. Es muss also Herbst sein. Wenigstens dort, wo traurige Frauen von uns wissen.

*R*iding, *riding*, riding, through the day, through the night, through the day.

Riding, riding, riding.

And courage is grown so weary, and longing so great. There are no hills any more, hardly a tree. Nothing dares stand up. Alien huts crouch thirstily by mired springs. Nowhere a tower. And always the same picture. One has two eyes too many. Only in the night sometimes one seems to know the road. Perhaps we always retrace by night the stretch we have won laboriously in the foreign sun? Maybe. The sun is heavy, as with us deep in summer at home. But we took our leave in summer. The women's dresses shone long out of the green. And we have been riding long. So it must be autumn. At least there, where sorrowful women know of us.

*D*er *von Langenau* rückt im Sattel und sagt: "Herr Marquis . . ."

Sein Nachbar, der kleine feine Franzose, hat erst drei Tage lang gesprochen und gelacht. Jetzt weiss er nichts mehr. Er ist wie ein Kind, das schlafen möchte. Staub bleibt auf seinem feinen weissen Spitzenkragen liegen; er merkt es nicht. Er wird langsam welk in seinem samtenen Sattel.

Aber der von Langenau lächelt und sagt: "Ihr habt seltsame Augen, Herr Marquis. Gewiss seht Ihr Eurer Mutter ähnlich—"

Da blüht der Kleine noch einmal auf und stäubt seinen Kragen ab und ist wie neu.

He of Langenau shifts in his saddle and says: "Marquis . . ."
His neighbor, the little fine Frenchman, has been talking
and laughing these three days. Now he has nothing more
to say. He is like a child that wants to sleep. Dust settles
on his fine white lace collar; he does not notice it. He is
slowly wilting in his velvet saddle.
But von Langenau smiles and says: "You have strange
eyes, Marquis. Surely you must look like your mother—"
At that the little fellow blossoms out again and dusts his
collar off and is like new.

Jemand erzählt von seiner Mutter. Ein Deutscher offenbar. Laut und langsam setzt er seine Worte. Wie ein Mädchen, das Blumen bindet, nachdenklich Blume um Blume probt und noch nicht weiss, was aus dem Ganzen wird—: so fügt er seine Worte. Zu Lust? Zu Leide? Alle lauschen. Sogar das Spucken hört auf. Denn es sind lauter Herren, die wissen, was sich gehört. Und wer das Deutsche nicht kann in dem Haufen, der versteht es auf einmal, fühlt einzelne Worte: "Abends" . . . "Klein war . . . "

Someone is telling of his mother. A German evidently. Loud and slow he sets his words. As a girl, binding flowers, thoughtfully tests flower after flower, not yet knowing what the whole will come to—: so he fits his words. For joy? For sorrow? All listen. Even the spitting stops. For these are gentlemen every one, who know what is proper. And whoever speaks no German in the party suddenly understands it, feels individual words: "At evening" . . . "was little" . . .

$\mathcal{D}$*a sind sie* alle einander nah, diese Herren, die aus Frankreich kommen und aus Burgund, aus den Niederlanden, aus Kärntens Tälern, von den böhmischen Burgen und vom Kaiser Leopold. Denn was der Eine erzählt, das haben auch sie erfahren und gerade so. Als ob es nur *eine* Mutter gäbe . . .

N̄ow are they all close to one another, these gentlemen that come out of France and out of Burgundy, out of the Netherlands, out of Carinthia's valleys, from the castles of Bohemia and from the Emperor Leopold. For what this one tells they too have experienced, and just as he has. As though there were but *one* mother . .

*S*o *reitet man* in den Abend hinein, in irgend einen Abend. Man schweigt wieder, aber man hat die lichten Worte mit. Da hebt der Marquis den Helm ab. Seine dunklen Haare sind weich und, wie er das Haupt senkt, dehnen sie sich frauenhaft auf seinem Nacken. Jetzt erkennt auch der von Langenau: Fern ragt etwas in den Glanz hinein, etwas Schlankes, Dunkles. Eine einsame Säule, halbverfallen. Und wie sie lange vorüber sind, später, fällt ihm ein, dass das eine Madonna war.

So they ride into the evening, into any evening. They are silent again, but they have the bright words with them. The Marquis doffs his helmet. His dark hair is soft, and, as he bows his head, it spreads like a woman's about his neck. Now von Langenau too is aware: Far off something rises into the radiance, something slender, dark. A lonely column, half ruined. And when they are long past, later, it occurs to him that that was a Madonna.

Wachtfeuer. Man sitzt rundherum und wartet. Wartet, dass einer singt. Aber man ist so müd. Das rote Licht ist schwer. Es liegt auf den staubigen Schuhn. Es kriecht bis an die Kniee, es schaut in die gefalteten Hände hinein. Es hat keine Flügel. Die Gesichter sind dunkel. Dennoch leuchten eine Weile die Augen des kleinen Franzosen mit eigenem Licht. Er hat eine kleine Rose geküsst, und nun darf sie weiterwelken an seiner Brust. Der von Langenau hat es gesehen, weil er nicht schlafen kann. Er denkt: Ich habe keine Rose, keine.

Dann singt er. Und das ist ein altes trauriges Lied, das zu Hause die Mädchen auf den Feldern singen, im Herbst, wenn die Ernten zu Ende gehen.

Watch-fire. They sit round about and wait. Wait for some-one to sing. But they are so tired. The red light is heavy. It lies on the dusty boots. It crawls up to the knees, it peers into the folded hands. It has no wings. The faces are dark. Even so, the eyes of the little Frenchman glow for a while with a light of their own. He has kissed a little rose, and now it may wither on upon his breast. Von Langenau has seen it, because he cannot sleep. He thinks: I have no rose, none.

Then he sings. And it is an old sad song that at home the girls in the fields sing, in the fall, when the harvests are coming to an end.

Sagt der kleine Marquis: "Ihr seid sehr jung, Herr?"
Und der von Langenau, in Trauer halb und halb im
Trotz: "Achtzehn." Dann schweigen sie.
Später fragt der Franzose: "Habt Ihr auch eine Braut
daheim, Herr Junker?"
"Ihr?" gibt der von Langenau zurück.
"Sie ist blond wie Ihr."
Und sie schweigen wieder, bis der Deutsche ruft: "Aber
zum Teufel, warum sitzt Ihr denn dann im Sattel und
reitet durch dieses giftige Land den türkischen Hunden
entgegen?"
Der Marquis lächelt. "Um wiederzukehren."
Und der von Langenau wird traurig. Er denkt an ein
blondes Mädchen, mit dem er spielte. Wilde Spiele. Und
er möchte nach Hause, für einen Augenblick nur, nur für
so lange, als es braucht um die Worte zu sagen: "Magda-
lena—dass ich immer *so war*, verzeih!"
Wie—war? denkt der junge Herr.—Und sie sind weit.

Says the little Marquis: "You are very young, sir?"
And von Langenau, in sorrow half and half defiant:
"Eighteen." Then they are silent.
Later the Frenchman asks: "Have you too a bride at
home, Junker?"
"You?" returns von Langenau.
"She is blond like you."
And they are silent again until the German cries: "But
then why the devil do you sit in the saddle and ride
through this poisonous country to meet the Turkish
dogs?"
The Marquis smiles: "In order to come back again."
And von Langenau grows sad. He thinks of a blond girl
with whom he played. Wild games. And he would like
to go home, for an instant only, only for so long as it
takes to say the words: "Magdalena—my having always
been *like that*, forgive!"
Like—*what?* thinks the young man.—And they are far
away.

Einmal, am Morgen, ist ein Reiter da, und dann ein zweiter, vier, zehn. Ganz in Eisen, gross. Dann tausend dahinter: das Heer.

Man muss sich trennen.

"Kehrt glücklich heim, Herr Marquis.—"

"Die Maria schützt Euch, Herr Junker."

Und sie können nicht voneinander. Sie sind Freunde auf einmal, Brüder. Haben einander mehr zu vertrauen; denn sie wissen schon so viel Einer vom Andern. Sie zögern. Und ist Hast und Hufschlag um sie. Da streift der Marquis den grossen rechten Handschuh ab. Er holt die kleine Rose hervor, nimmt ihr ein Blatt. Als ob man eine Hostie bricht.

"Das wird Euch beschirmen, Lebt wohl."

Der von Langenau staunt. Lange schaut er dem Franzosen nach. Dann schiebt er das fremde Blatt unter den Waffenrock. Und es treibt auf und ab auf den Wellen seines Herzens. Hornruf. Er reitet zum Heer, der Junker. Er lächelt traurig: ihn schützt eine fremde Frau.

One day, at morning, a horseman appears, and then a second, four, ten. All in iron, huge. Then a thousand behind: the army.

One must separate.

"Return safely home, Marquis—"

"The Virgin protects you, Junker."

And they cannot part. They are friends of a sudden, brothers. Have more to confide in each other; for they already know so much each of the other. They linger. And there's haste and hoofbeat about them. Then the Marquis strips off his great right glove. He fetches out the little rose, takes a petal from it. As one would break a host.

"That will safeguard you. Fare well."

Von Langenau is surprised. He gazes long after the Frenchman. Then he shoves the foreign petal under his tunic. And it rises and falls on the waves of his heart. Bugle-call. He rides to the army, the Junker. He smiles sadly: a woman he does not know is protecting him.

Ein Tag durch den Tross. Flüche, Farben, Lachen—: davon blendet das Land. Kommen bunte Buben gelaufen. Raufen und Rufen. Kommen Dirnen mit purpurnen Hüten im flutenden Haar. Winken. Kommen Knechte, schwarzeisern wie wandernde Nacht. Packen die Dirnen heiss, dass ihnen die Kleider zerreissen. Drücken sie an den Trommelrand. Und von der wilderen Gegenwehr hastiger Hände werden die Trommeln wach, wie im Traum poltern sie, poltern. Und abends halten sie ihm Laternen her, seltsame: Wein, leuchtend in eisernen Hauben. Wein? Oder Blut? – Wer kanns unterscheiden?

A *day through* the baggage-train. Curses, colors, laughter —: the countryside is dazzling with it. Come gay-clad boys a-running. Brawling and calling. Come wenches with crimson hats amid their full-flowing hair. Beckonings. Come men-at-arms, black-iron as wandering night. Seize the hussies hotly, that their clothes tear. Press them against the drum's edge. And at the wilder struggling of hasty hands the drums awake; as in a dream they rumble, rumble —. And at evening they hold out lanterns to him, strange ones: wine, gleaming in iron headpieces. Wine? Or blood? — Who can distinguish?

Endlich vor Spork. Neben seinem Schimmel ragt der Graf. Sein langes Haar hat den Glanz des Eisens. Der von Langenau hat nicht gefragt. Er erkennt den General, schwingt sich vom Ross und verneigt sich in einer Wolke Staub. Er bringt ein Schreiben mit, das ihn empfehlen soll beim Grafen. Der aber befiehlt: "Lies mir den Wisch." Und seine Lippen haben sich nicht bewegt. Er braucht sie nicht dazu; sind zum Fluchen gerade gut genug. Was drüber hinaus ist, redet die Rechte. Punktum. Und man sieht es ihr an. Der junge Herr ist längst zu Ende. Er weiss nicht mehr, wo er steht. Der Spork ist vor Allem. Sogar der Himmel ist fort. Da sagt Spork, der grosse General:

"Cornet."

Und das ist viel.

At last in Spork's presence. Beside his white horse the Count towers. His long hair has the gleam of iron.

Von Langenau has not asked. He recognizes the General, swings from his horse and bows in a cloud of dust. He brings a letter commending him to the Count's favor. But the Count commands: "Read me the scrawl." And his lips have not moved. He does not need them for this; they're just good enough for cursing. Anything further his right hand says. Period. And one can tell by the look of it.—The young man has finished long ago. He no longer knows where he is standing. Spork is in front of everything. Even the sky is gone. Then Spork, the great General, says:

"Cornet."

And that is much.

Die Kompagnie liegt jenseits der Raab. Der von Langenau
reitet hin, allein. Ebene. Abend. Der Beschlag vorn am
Sattel glänzt durch den Staub. Und dann steigt der Mond.
Er sieht es an seinen Händen.
Er träumt.
Aber da schreit es ihn an.
Schreit, schreit,
zerreisst ihm den Traum.
Das ist keine Eule. Barmherzigkeit:
der einzige Baum
schreit ihn an:
Mann!
Und er schaut: es bäumt sich. Es bäumt sich ein
Leib den Baum entlang, und ein junges Weib,
blutig und bloss,
fällt ihn an: Mach mich los!

Und er springt hinab in das schwarze Grün
und durchhaut die heissen Stricke;
und er sieht ihre Blicke glühn
und ihre Zähne beissen.

Lacht sie?

Ihn graust.
Und er sitzt schon zu Ross
und jagt in die Nacht. Blutige
Schnüre fest in der Faust.

The company is lying beyond the Raab. Langenau rides
   towards it, alone. Level land. Evening. The studdings of
   his saddle-bow gleam through the dust. And then the
   moon rises. He sees that by his hands.
He dreams.
But then something shrieks at him.
Shrieks, shrieks,
rends his dream.
That is no owl. Mercy:
the only tree
shrieks at him:
man!
And he looks: something rears—a body rears itself
against the tree, and a young woman,
bloody and bare,
assails him: Let me loose!

And down he springs into the black green
and hews the hot ropes through;
and he sees her glances glow
and her teeth bite.

Is she laughing?

He shudders.
And already he sits his horse
and chases into the
night. Bloody ties fast in his fist.

*D*er *von Langenau* schreibt einen Brief, ganz in Gedanken. Langsam malt er mit grossen, ernsten, aufrechten Lettern:
"Meine gute Mutter,
seid stolz: Ich trage die Fahne,
seid ohne Sorge: Ich trage die Fahne,
habt mich lieb: Ich trage die Fahne—"

Dann steckt er den Brief zu sich in den Waffenrock, an die heimlichste Stelle, neben das Rosenblatt. Und denkt: er wird bald duften davon. Und denkt: Vielleicht findet ihn einmal Einer . . . Und denkt: . . . ; denn der Feind ist nah.

Von Langenau is writing a letter, deep in thought. Slowly he traces in great, earnest, upright letters:

"My good mother,
"be proud: I carry the flag,
"be free of care: I carry the flag,
"love me: I carry the flag—"

Then he puts the letter away inside his tunic, in the most secret place, beside the roseleaf. And thinks: It will soon take on that fragrance. And thinks: Perhaps someone will find it someday . . . And thinks: . . . ; for the enemy is near.

Sie reiten über einen erschlagenen Bauer. Er hat die Augen weit offen und etwas spiegelt sich drin; kein Himmel. Später heulen Hunde. Es kommt also ein Dorf, endlich. Und über den Hütten steigt steinern ein Schloss. Breit hält sich ihnen die Brücke hin. Gross wird das Tor. Hoch willkommt das Horn. Horch: Poltern, Klirren und Hundegebell! Wiehern im Hof, Hufschlag und Ruf.

They ride over a slain peasant. His eyes are wide open and something is mirrored in them; no heaven. Later hounds howl. So a village is coming, at last. And above the hovels stonily rises a castle. Broad the bridge presents itself before them. Great grows the gate. High welcomes the horn. Hark: rumble, clatter, and barking of dogs! Neighing in the courtyard, hoof-beat and hailing.

*R*ast! Gast sein einmal. Nicht immer selbst seine Wünsche bewirten mit karglicher Kost. Nicht immer feindlich nach allem fassen; einmal sich alles geschehen lassen und wissen: Was geschieht, ist gut. Auch der Mut muss einmal sich strecken und sich am Saume seidener Decken in sich selber überschlagen. Nicht immer Soldat sein. Einmal die Locken offen tragen und den weiten offenen Kragen und in seidenen Sesseln sitzen und bis in die Fingerspitzen so:—nach dem Bad sein. Und wieder erst lernen, was Frauen sind. Und wie die weissen tun und wie die blauen sind; was für Hände sie haben, wie sie ihr Lachen singen, wenn blonde Knaben die schönen Schalen bringen, von saftigen Früchten schwer.

*R*est! To be a guest for once. Not always oneself to supply one's wishes with scanty fare. Not always to seize things, enemy-like; for once to let things happen to one and to know: what happens is good. Courage too must stretch out for once and at the hem of silken covers turn over on itself. Not always to be a soldier. For once to wear one's hair loose and the broad open collar and to sit upon silken settles and be to the very fingertips as . . . after the bath. And to begin again learning what women are. And how the white ones do and how the blue ones are; what sort of hands they have, how they sing their laughter, when blond boys bring the beautiful bowls weighted with juice-laden fruits.

*A*ls *Mahl beganns*. Und ist ein Fest geworden, kaum weiss man wie. Die hohen Flammen flackten, die Stimmen schwirrten, wirre Lieder klirrten aus Glas und Glanz, und endlich aus den reifgewordnen Takten: entsprang der Tanz. Und alle riss er hin. Das war ein Wellenschlagen in den Sälen, ein Sich-Begegnen und ein Sich-Erwählen, ein Abschiednehmen und ein Wiederfinden, ein Glanzgeniessen und ein Lichterblinden und ein Sich-Wiegen in den Sommerwinden, die in den Kleidern warmer Frauen sind.

Aus dunklem Wein und Tausend Rosen rinnt die Stunde rauschend in den Traum der Nacht.

It began as a feast. And became a festival, one hardly knows how. The high flames flared, voices whirred, tangled songs jangled out of glass and glitter, and at last from the ripe-grown measures—forth sprang the dance. And swept them all away. That was a beating of waves in the halls, a meeting together and a choosing of each other, a parting with each other and a finding again, a rejoicing in the radiance and a blinding in the light and a swaying in the summer winds that are in the costumes of warm women.

Out of dark wine and a thousand roses runs the hour rushing into the dream of night.

Und Einer steht und staunt in diese Pracht. Und er ist so geartet, dass er wartet, ob er erwacht. Denn nur im Schlafe schaut man solchen Staat und solche Feste solcher Frauen: ihre kleinste Geste ist eine Falte, fallend in Brokat. Sie bauen Stunden auf aus silbernen Gesprächen, und manchmal heben sie die Hände so—, und du musst meinen, dass sie irgendwo, wo du nicht hinreichst, sanfte Rosen brächen, die du nicht siehst. Und da träumst du: Geschmückt sein mit ihnen und anders beglückt sein und dir eine Krone verdienen für deine Stirne, die leer ist.

And one there is who stands and marvels at this splendor. And he is so made that he waits whether to come awake. Because in sleep alone one sees such state and such festivals of such women: their slightest gesture is a fold falling in brocade. They build up hours out of silvery discourses, and sometimes lift their hands up: so—, and you must think that somewhere whither you cannot reach, they break soft roses that you do not see. And then you dream: to be adorn'd with these and be elsewise blest, and earning a crown for your brow that is empty.

Einer, der weisse Seide trägt, erkennt, dass er nicht erwachen
kann; denn er ist wach und verwirrt von Wirklichkeit.
So flieht er bange in den Traum und steht im Park, einsam
im schwarzen Park. Und das Fest ist fern. Und das Licht
lügt. Und die Nacht ist nahe um ihn und kühl. Und er
fragt eine Frau, die sich zu ihm neigt:
"Bist Du die Nacht?"
Sie lächelt.
Und da schämt er sich für sein weisses Kleid.
Und möchte weit und allein und in Waffen sein.
Ganz in Waffen.

One, who wears white silk, now knows that he cannot wake; for he is awake and bewildered with reality. So he flees fearfully into the dream and stands in the park, lonely in the black park. And the feast is far. And the light lies. And the night is near about him and cool. And he asks a woman, who leans to him:
"Are you the night?"
She smiles.
And at that he is ashamed for his white dress.
And would be far and alone and in armor.
All in armor.

Hast Du vergessen, dass Du mein Page bist für diesen Tag? Verlässest Du mich? Wo gehst Du hin? Dein weisses Kleid gibt mir Dein Recht—."

* * *

"Sehnt es Dich nach Deinem rauhen Rock?"

* * *

"Frierst Du? — Hast Du Heimweh?"
Die Gräfin lächelt.
Nein. Aber das ist nur, weil das Kindsein ihm von den Schultern gefallen ist, dieses sanfte dunkle Kleid. Wer hat es fortgenommen? "Du?" fragt er mit einer Stimme, die er noch nicht gehört hat. "Du!"
Und nun ist nichts an ihm. Und er ist nackt wie ein Heiliger. Hell und schlank.

*H*ave you forgotten that you are my page for this day? Are you leaving me? Where are you going? Your white dress gives me right over you—."

* * *

"Do you long for your coarse coat?"

* * *

"Are you cold? — Are you homesick?"
The Countess smiles.
No. But that is only because the being a child has fallen from his shoulders, that soft dark dress. Who has taken it away? "You?" he asks in a voice he has not yet heard. "You!"
And now he has nothing on. And he is naked as a saint. Bright and slender.

Langsam lischt das Schloss aus. Alle sind schwer: müde oder verliebt oder trunken. Nach so vielen leeren, langen Feldnächten: Betten. Breite eichene Betten. Da betet sichs anders als in der lumpigen Furche unterwegs, die, wenn man einschlafen will, wie ein Grab wird.

"Herrgott, wie Du willst!"

Kürzer sind die Gebete im Bett.

Aber inniger.

Slowly the castle lights go out. Everyone is heavy: tired or in love or drunk. After so many empty, long nights in the field: beds. Broad oaken beds. Here one prays otherwise than in a wretched furrow on the way, which, as one falls asleep, becomes like a grave.

"Lord God, as thou willest!"

Shorter are the prayers in bed.

But more heartfelt.

*D*ie *Turmstube* ist dunkel.

Aber sie leuchten sich ins Gesicht mit ihrem Lächeln.
Sie tasten vor sich her wie Blinde und finden den Andern
wie eine Tür. Fast wie Kinder, die sich vor der Nacht
ängstigen, drängen sie sich in einander ein. Und doch
fürchten sie sich nicht. Da ist nichts, was gegen sie wäre:
kein Gestern, kein Morgen; denn die Zeit ist eingestürzt.
Und sie blühen aus ihren Trümmern.
Er fragt nicht: "Dein Gemahl?"
Sie fragt nicht: "Dein Namen?"
Sie haben sich ja gefunden, um einander ein neues Ge-
schlecht zu sein.
Sie werden sich hundert neue Namen geben und einander
alle wieder abnehmen, wie man einen Ohrring abnimmt.

The tower room is dark.

But they light each other's faces with their smiles. They grope before them like blind people and find each the other as they would a door. Almost like children that dread the night, they press close into each other. And yet they are not afraid. There is nothing that might be against them: no yesterday, no morrow; for time is shattered. And they flower from its ruins.

He does not ask: "Your husband?"

She does not ask: "Your name?"

For indeed they have found each other, to be unto themselves a new generation.

They will give each other a hundred new names and take them all off again, gently, as one takes an ear-ring off.

Im Vorsaal über einem Sessel hängt der Waffenrock, das Bandelier und der Mantel von dem von Langenau. Seine Handschuhe liegen auf dem Fussboden. Seine Fahne steht steil, gelehnt an das Fensterkreuz. Sie ist schwarz und schlank. Draussen jagt ein Sturm über den Himmel hin und macht Stücke aus der Nacht, weisse und schwarze. Der Mondschein geht wie ein langer Blitz vorbei, und die reglose Fahne hat unruhige Schatten. Sie träumt.

In the antechamber over a settle hangs the tunic, the bandolier and the cloak of him of Langenau. His gloves lie on the floor. His flag stands steeply, leaned against the window-cross. It is black and slender. Outside a storm drives over the sky, making pieces of the night, white ones and black ones. The moonlight goes by like a long lightning-flash, and the unstirring flag has restless shadows. It dreams.

War ein Fenster offen? Ist der Sturm im Haus? Wer schlägt die Türen zu? Wer geht durch die Zimmer?—Lass. Wer es auch sei. Ins Turmgemach findet er nicht. Wie hinter hundert Türen ist dieser grosse Schlaf, den zwei Menschen gemeinsam haben; so gemeinsam wie *eine* Mutter oder *einen* Tod.

Was a window open? Is the storm in the house? Who is slamming the doors? Who goes through the rooms?—Let be. No matter who. Into the tower room he will not find his way. As behind a hundred doors is this great sleep two people have in common; as much in common as *one* mother or *one* death.

Ist das der Morgen? Welche Sonne geht auf? Wie gross ist die Sonne? Sind das Vögel? Ihre Stimmen sind überall.
Alles ist hell, aber es ist kein Tag.
Alles ist laut, aber es sind nicht Vogelstimmen.
Das sind die Balken, die leuchten. Das sind die Fenster, die schrein. Und sie schrein, rot, in die Feinde hinein, die draussen stehn im flackernden Land, schrein: Brand.
Und mit zerrissenem Schlaf im Gesicht drängen sich alle, halb Eisen, halb nackt, von Zimmer zu Zimmer, von Trakt zu Trakt und suchen die Treppe.
Und mit verschlagenem Atem stammeln die Hörner im Hof:
Sammeln, sammeln!
Und bebende Trommeln.

Is this the morning? What sun is rising? How big is the sun? Are those birds? Their voices are everywhere.

All is bright, but it is not day.

All is loud, but not with the voices of birds.

It is the timbers that shine. It is the windows that scream. And they scream, red, into the foes that stand outside in the flickering land, scream: Fire!

And with torn sleep in their faces they all throng through, half iron, half naked, from room to room, from wing to wing, and seek the stair.

And with broken breath horns stammer in the court: Muster, muster!

And quaking drums.

Aber die Fahne ist nicht dabei.
    Rufe: Cornet!
    Rasende Pferde, Gebete, Geschrei,
    Flüche: Cornet!
    Eisen an Eisen, Befehl und Signal;
    Stille: Cornet!
    Und noch ein Mal: Cornet!
    Und heraus mit der brausenden Reiterei.

* * *

Aber die Fahne ist nicht dabei.

*B*ut *the flag* is not there.
  Cries: Cornet!
  Careering horses, prayers, shouts,
  Curses: Cornet!
  Iron on iron, signal, command;
  Stillness: Cornet!
  And once again: Cornet!
  And away with the thundering cavalcade.

      * * *

But the flag is not there.

Er läuft um die Wette mit brennenden Gängen, durch Türen, die ihn glühend umdrängen, über Treppen, die ihn versengen, bricht er aus aus dem rasenden Bau. Auf seinen Armen trägt er die Fahne wie eine weisse, bewusstlose Frau. Und er findet ein Pferd, und es ist wie ein Schrei: über alles dahin und an allem vorbei, auch an den Seinen. Und da kommt auch die Fahne wieder zu sich, und niemals war sie so königlich; und jetzt sehn sie sie alle, fern voran, und erkennen den hellen, helmlosen Mann und erkennen die Fahne . . .

Aber da fängt sie zu scheinen an, wirft sich hinaus und wird gross und rot . . .

* * *

Da brennt ihre Fahne mitten im Feind, und sie jagen ihr nach.

He is running a race with burning halls, through doors that press him close, red-hot, over stairs that scorch him, he breaks forth out of the raging pile. Upon his arms he carries the flag like a white, insensible woman. And he finds a horse, and it's like a cry: away over all, passing everything by, even his own men. And then the flag comes to itself again, and it has never been so kingly; and now they all see it, far in the van, and know the shining, helmetless man and know the flag . . .

But, behold, it begins to glow, flings itself out and grows wide and red . . .

* * *

Their flag is aflame in the enemy's midst, and they gallop after.

*D*er *von Langenau* ist tief im Feind, aber ganz allein. Der Schrecken hat um ihn einen runden Raum gemacht, und er hält, mitten drin, unter seiner langsam verlodernden Fahne.

Langsam, fast nachdenklich, schaut er um sich. Es ist viel Fremdes, Buntes vor ihm. Gärten—denkt er und lächelt. Aber da fühlt er, dass Augen ihn halten, und erkennt Männer und weiss, dass es die heidnischen Hunde sind—: und wirft sein Pferd mitten hinein.

Aber, als es jetzt hinter ihm zusammenschlägt, sind es doch wieder Gärten, und die sechzehn runden Säbel, die auf ihn zuspringen, Strahl um Strahl, sind ein Fest.

Eine lachende Wasserkunst.

He of Langenau is deep in the enemy, but all alone. Terror
has ringed a space around him, and he halts, in the very
middle, under the slowly dying flare of his flag.

Slowly, almost reflectively, he gazes about him. There is
much that is strange, motley before him. Gardens—he
thinks and smiles. But then he feels that eyes are holding
him and is aware of men and knows that these are the
heathen dogs—: and casts his horse into their midst.

But, as he is now closed in on from behind, they are
indeed gardens again, and the sixteen curved sabres that
leap upon him, flash on flash, are a festival.

A laughing fountain.

$\mathcal{D}$*er Waffenrock* ist im Schlosse verbrannt, der Brief und das Rosenblatt einer fremden Frau.—

Im nächsten Frühjahr (es kam traurig und kalt) ritt ein Kurier des Freiherrn von Pirovano langsam in Langenau ein. Dort hat er eine alte Frau weinen sehen.

The tunic was burnt in the castle, the letter and the rose-leaf of an unknown woman.—

In the spring of the next year (it came sad and cold) a courier of the Baron of Pirovano rode slowly into Langenau. There he saw an old woman weep.

CONTINENTAL LITERATURE IN NORTON LIBRARY
AND LIVERIGHT PAPERBACK

NORTON CRITICAL EDITIONS

Dostoevsky, Feodor *The Brothers Karamazov* (Matlaw, Ed.)
                    Crime and Punishment (Gibian, Ed.)
Flaubert, Gustave *Madame Bovary* (De Man, Ed.)
Goethe, Johann Wolfgang von *Faust* (Arndt, Tr.; Hamlin, Ed.)
Ibsen, Henrik *The Wild Duck* (Christiani, Tr. and Ed.)
Stendhal *Red and Black* (Adams, Tr. and Ed.)
Tolstoy, Leo *Anna Karenina* (Gibian, Ed.)
             War and Peace (Gibian, Ed.)
Turgenev, Ivan *Fathers and Sons* (Matlaw, Ed.)
Voltaire *Candide* (Adams, Tr. and Ed.)